Tiny fragments of a life redacted

Peter Chua

Presentation by *BookLeaf Publishing*

Web: www.bookleafpub.com

E-mail: info@bookleafpub.com

ISBN: 9789357214636

First edition 2022

For my mum

No words are needed

PREFACE

All bad poetry springs from genuine feeling.
- Oscar Wilde

A meta poem

What I want to write

Is pulled in different directions

Voices in my head

Surround to take it apart

They won't stop the chatter

To leave me just be

Who do you follow

Take flight to the light or

Dive down into darkness

Shadows are everywhere

The voices carry my pen

Towards some unrelenting goal

Not sure what it could be

But I hope someday

You will be able to read it

Sanctuary

Songbirds wake the Sun

As she stretches her arms

Singing a bright melody

To signal a new start

Their love song is joined

By man and machine

The growing chorus

Of the morning rush

Bodies in motion collide

In this communal dance

They move in a state

That's not fully awake

Yet there is stillness

An oasis I have found

A sense of tranquillity

Away from the crowd

It only shows itself

In a few stolen moments

With the fresh sweet scent

Of my first morning cup

And then it is gone

My mind hides it away

As machinations whirr on

Ready to face the day

The journey

A train of thought at journey's end

The notion of a different life

A recurring anticipation

Contemplating adventures past

What was lost can yet be found

A train of thought at journey's end

A traversal of rediscovery

The commute to a new pilgrimage

A recurring anticipation

A derailment of this present trip

An accident waiting to happen

A train of thought at journey's end

A myriad of choices to be made

At the station interchange

A recurring anticipation

Life's wandering rambles on

The final destination still unknown

A train of thought at journey's end

A recurring anticipation

Washing machine

She places his dirty laundry

Deep into the drum

Her household ritual

To wash away the scum

She leaves enough space

For lots of detergent

Soaking through lies

Won't be a deterrent

She picks a strong cycle

And watches it spin

Ah..domestic bliss

Infidelity cannot win

Yoga is like bread

Yoga is like bread

Best served fresh

To start the day

Bringing joy

A brief getaway

Twisting, kneading

Let the breath in

Shapes the body

Heat rises within

Yoga is like bread

A spiritual experience

Awakening the senses

Where one receives

No false pretenses

Tranquil fulfillment

Cultivating growth

A sweet contentment

Namaste… on the go

Tiny fragments about food

"Cinnamon buns"

Big swirls of sweetness

Sassy with a little spice

A star attraction

Always royal in presence

Handy for a rebel war

"Lemon cake"

Citrus tears perk up

With every bitter morsel

Revenge exacted

"Ready meal"

Flat packed emptiness

Seals in a sensory taste

The sound of dinner

Ringing to ward off silence

A banquet laid out for one

Tiny fragments about drink

"Coffee"

Black gems of the world

Unearthed from exotic lands

Creates a rich brew

Inspires life and romance

Treasured by everyday man

"Bubble tea"

Sweet pearls of wisdom

Bubbling over on warm days

Eschewing insight

"Irn Bru"

Copper concoction

Radiates atomic pep

Packs a sugared punch

After long nights in stasis

A cheap thrill for everyone

Empty glass

The bar's last orders ring

A death knell for the heart

The last drop unspoken

Drunk

Tiny cracks reflect

Regrets left in place

My indecision of decision

Unmade

The stain of your lips

Smudged still remains

An intimation of the act

Complete

Swirling in sadness

I am an empty glass

Waiting for nobody

Alone

Dancing queens

Alpine stilettos

Towers over cha-cha heels

Readies for battle

Across glittery landscapes

To confront their waterloo

Beating of drums rise

A call to arms on the floor

All the fires are lit

Heralding the queens' approach

As houses sashay to war

Rhythms of the night

Explode in aural colour

Their majestic struts

Slaying in infinite moves

Brings murder on the dancefloor

And the beat goes on

Pulsating across the land

Our divas unite

The world of smoke and mirrors

Saved by the sounds of disco

It

Everybody wants it

But nobody's getting it

Making the effort

Swiping left to right

Perpetual anticipation

Leads to nowhere

Fingers do the talking

Click snap send

Never once a hello

Words are too precious

A squiggly emoji

Expresses the feels

Convenience gives hope

Offering more possibilities

A warm fuzzy sensation

Everybody is waiting

Nobody wants it

Intimacy

Tiny poems about love

"First crush"

Frog in throat jumps out

When love's first sight approaches

Silence still surrounds

"Cuddle therapy"

Arms wrapped around arms

Bodies warming side by side

Silence is golden

In the comfort of strangers

Looking for a connection

"Love"

Fractured

Little pieces

The remnants of my heart

Will you be able to fix it

Maybe

Tiny fragments about lust

"Cruising"

Between the trees

Speechless

Feel the fever

Swelter

Eyes precede

Steer the need

They meet

Free

"Lust, caution"

Time in slow motion

Ardent looks across the hall

In the mood for love

Sparks without a single touch

Never fully ignited

"Lingerie"

Lust calls through the net

Enticing me to your web

My hands are tangled

As they struggle to break through

Ensuing passion is lost

Maryhill canal

Grass shimmers along the path

As dusk comes out to play

A much-needed distraction

To the dank darkness beneath

Children's laughter fades

Tucked away for tea

Overtaken by neon cyclists

Dinging their way past

The aromatic scent of spices

Entices from houseboats far

A comforting reminder

The walk home is almost done

Tiny fragments about Scotland

"Loch Leven"

Calm waters belie

Flights of nature that surround

Life's new wings will soar

"Rannoch Moor"

Tears fall endlessly

On lonely fields with no end

Silent in sadness

"St Kilda"

Lonely isles stand tall

Guards the gates with wails and tears

A lost paradise

Tiny fragments about Christmas

"Christmas dinner"

Happy pleasantries

Make for light entertainment

Revealing nothing

To hide mischief in plain sight

Pernicious intimation

"Secret Santa"

Festive tidings bring

Gifts for a game of roulette

The croupier spins

See what the pocket will win

Before moving on to craps

31

"Christmas pudding"

Sweet ball on fire

Handed down through the ages

Ensures peace and joy

When warring parties gather

They truce in treacly delight

Paternal instinct

My mind falls through the cracks

Listening to sounds below

Of a father and a child

Connection in its ebb and flow

Their kindred song uplifts

And leaves me reflecting

What my life would have been

If only you had stopped wandering

But how could we begin

When you were never there

Singing our first duet

Became a solo affair

So instead I developed

A steely sense of distance

Your wayward independence

Grew my acoustic resistance

But now things are different

To soothe paternal rhythms

A meow's a nurturing sound

I guess that will be enough

Performance

Lights camera action

I am ready for my close-up

A face that could launch a thousand ships

Smiling with the eyes of Horus

I can be anything you want me to be

A new persona at the flash of your bulb

Little boy blue

A mother of one

I like what you like

Whatever makes you happy

A satisfied customer

My sense of achievement

When the floodlights are off the stage bare

Who am I without you

Persona non-grata

No one

Lost

Namesake

My name was given

After the first saint

Rock of the church

A firm foundation

Which others relied on

Although chinks

Began to show

Stones and name calling

Little by little

Have chipped it away

Once a mountain

Proud and tall

Lies exposed

Worn down to

A mere pebble

Maybe the name

Should be changed

Friendship lament

The aura of feeling

Shades of blue and grey

Your smile overshadows

White clouds in the sky

Words do not connect

Like they used to do

Listening to you loads

An emotional gun

The scent of joy hides

Whenever you are near

A stench of decay

Rumbles my insides

My intuition now toxic

From an eternity with you

Things would be different

If only you had asked

A life redacted

This life I have lived

Has opened doors to great unknowns

From a small isle Raffles came upon

I was abandoned by comrades

Yet thrived on my own

While MTV played and the music died

A vision to the masses

I was on the bus

As shadows in the sky collided

Raining down fire and stone

A September memorialized

It was years later

I would set foot on site

Watching Obama claim

America would be great again

Not expecting to be trumped

By an orange-haired goon

I didn't stay long to reflect

Sought pastures new

Walked along the Great Wall

From China to Berlin

Only to see it crumble

To a thing called unification

I did a cabaret to celebrate

Became the fabulous Fei Fei

I never dragged so good

In this brief respite

Before I settled down

Into a life of domestic bliss

Seduced by Marilyn and a Cartier ring

I strived to be an ideal husband

And realized I didn't want one

It was an independent life

I wanted to lead

Outside Old Compton Street

Dancing to Gloria Gaynor

As I stood in solidarity

With brothers in arms dead

From a disease with a tiny name

When a nail bomb in the Admiral

Exploded just because lives exist

I globe trotted some more

Forever displaced

From shore and shore

Trailed after Incas at Machu Pichu

En route to Kathmandu and Tibet

I spoke to my inner senses

Was told the time was near

Better be home soon

I saw my mother fly

Left her body at the door

She smiled a last kiss to me

I knew what I had to do

This life I have lived

Has been happy sad

I have stopped running

To bed down filial roots

I will carry a portable paradise

With me instead

Home

Scent of white lilies

Unfurling peace

Petals of wings

Ready to fly

Light of dusk

Casts a shadow

On the portrait

Left behind

Stillness of air

A beautiful silence

The room is empty

Bar one

Taste of teardrops

Running dry

Exhales

A last sigh